# DREAM JOBS IN SCIENCE

CHRIS OXLADE

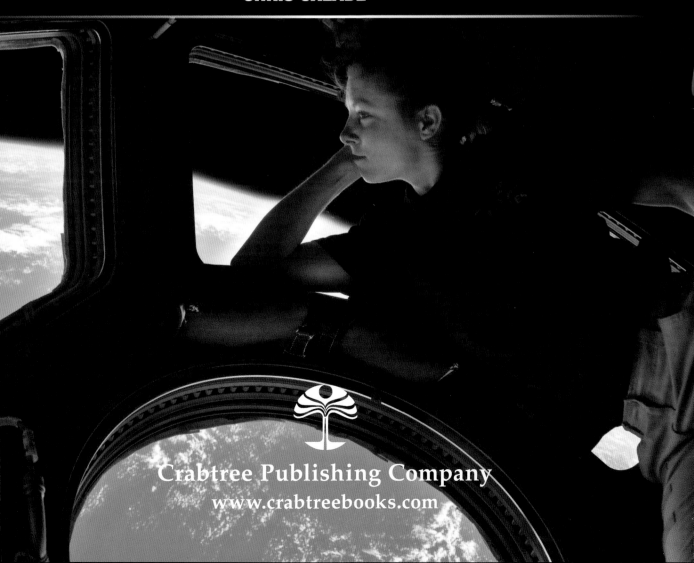

Crabtree Publishing Company
www.crabtreebooks.com

# Crabtree Publishing Company
www.crabtreebooks.com
1-800-387-7650

**Published in Canada**
616 Welland Ave.
St. Catharines, ON
L2M 5V6

**Published in the United States**
PMB 59051
350 Fifth Ave. 59th Floor
New York, NY 10118

**Published in 2017 by CRABTREE PUBLISHING COMPANY**

First published in 2016 by Wayland
(A division of Hachette Children's Books)
Copyright © Wayland 2016

**Author:**
Chris Oxlade

**Editors:**
Victoria Brooker
Jon Richards
Petrice Custance

**Designer:**
Darren Jordan

**Proofreader:**
Wendy Scavuzzo

**Print and production coordinator:**
Katherine Berti

**Photo credits**

1, 12 courtesy of NASA, 2, 22–23 Dreamstime.com/Endostock, 3, 14–15 Dreamstime.com/Stoyan Yotov, 4bl, 31br Dreamstime.com/Nordroden, 5t courtesy of NASA, 5cr Dreamstime.com/Songquan Deng, 6–7 All courtesy of NASA, 8–9 Dreamstime.com/Aniram, 9cr Dreamstime.com/MInervaStudio, 10-11 Dreamstime.com/Monkey Business Images, 10bl Dreamstime.com/Alexander Raths, 11tr CSIRO creative commons attribution, 12 All, 12–13 courtesy of NASA, 13cr Errabee creative commons attribution, 14c Dreamstime.com/Vesna Njagulj, 15br Dreamstime.com/Oleksandr Kontsevoi, 16–17 Dreamstime.com/Andreanita, 17tl Dreamstime.com/Tenedos, 17cr Daniel Leussler creative commons attribution, 18–19 Storm Talk creative commons attribution, 19tr courtesy of NOAA, 19bl Laubacht-commonswiki creative commons attribution, 20–21 Dreamstime.com/Pabla Hidalgo, 20bl, 21br courtesy of USGS, 22bl both courtesy of US Agricultural Research Service, 22c both courtesy of GloFish, 24–25 Dreamstime.com/Ruslan Glomanshin, 24bl TomCatX creative commons attribution, 26–27 Shutterstock.com/Pavel L Photo and Video, 26bl Dreamstime.com/Flynt, 27tl Reimundrost creative commons attribution, 27tr Thomas 89 creative commons attribution, 27bl Cosmed creative commons attribution, 28–29 Quibik creative commons attribution, 28bl Dreamstime.com/Xdrew, 29cr Soerfm creative commons attribution, 29bl Dreamstime.com/Grantotufo

**Library and Archives Canada Cataloguing in Publication**

Oxlade, Chris, author
    Dream jobs in science / Chris Oxlade.

(Cutting-edge careers in STEM)
Issued in print and electronic formats.
ISBN 978-0-7787-2965-5 (hardback).--
ISBN 978-0-7787-2973-0 (paperback).--
ISBN 978-1-4271-1862-2 (html)

    1. Science--Vocational guidance--Juvenile literature. I. Title.

Q147.H96 2016        j502.3        C2016-906640-1
                                   C2016-906641-X

**Library of Congress Cataloging-in-Publication Data**

Names: Oxlade, Chris.
Title: Dream jobs in science / Chris Oxlade.
Description: New York, N.Y. : Crabtree Publishing, 2017. |
    Series: Cutting-edge careers in STEM | Audience: Age 10-14. |
    Audience: Grade 7 to 8. | Includes index.
Identifiers: LCCN 2016045935 (print) |
    LCCN 2016046745 (ebook) |
    ISBN 9780778729655 (hardcover : alk. paper) |
    ISBN 9780778729730 (pbk. : alk. paper) |
    ISBN 9781427118622 (Electronic book text)
Subjects: LCSH: Science--Vocational guidance--Juvenile literature.
Classification: LCC Q147 .H94 2017 (print) | LCC Q147 (ebook) |
    DDC 502.3--dc23
LC record available at https://lccn.loc.gov/2016045935

Printed in Hong Kong/012017/BK20161024

# CONTENTS

## SCIENCE

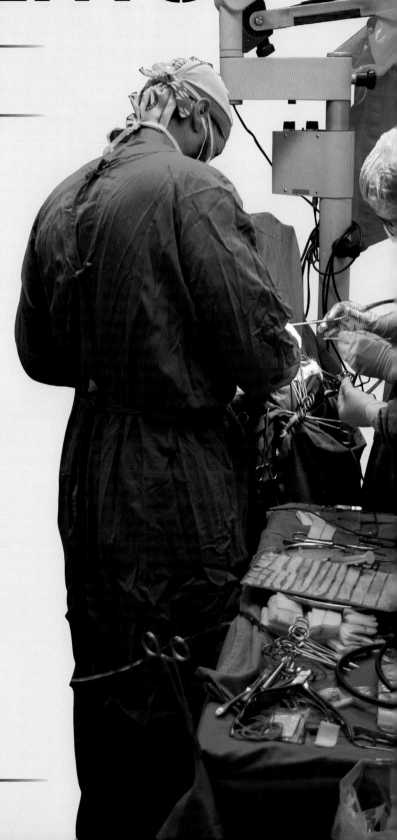

# JOBS IN SCIENCE

## QUALIFICATIONS IN SCIENCE CAN TAKE YOU FROM THE WILDS OF THE WORLD TO THE VERY EDGE OF SPACE!

Welcome to the world of working in science. Studying science is really worthwhile, because it opens doors to a whole range of interesting, exciting, unusual, and amazing jobs in science. Studying science doesn't mean you'll be stuck in a lab. There are jobs in space, astronomy, sports, and food production that you could get into. This book will help you find out what each job is all about, as well as the rewards of doing the job.

▼ Polar scientists provide vital data on the health and condition of the planet.

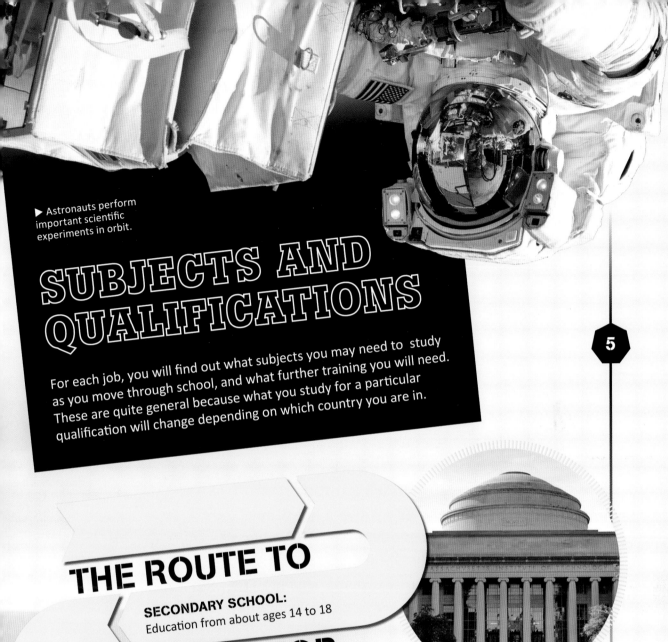

▶ Astronauts perform important scientific experiments in orbit.

# SUBJECTS AND QUALIFICATIONS

For each job, you will find out what subjects you may need to study as you move through school, and what further training you will need. These are quite general because what you study for a particular qualification will change depending on which country you are in.

## THE ROUTE TO A SCIENCE JOB

**SECONDARY SCHOOL:**
Education from about ages 14 to 18

**POST-SECONDARY:**
Studying for an **undergraduate** degree and a post-graduate degree, such as a **master's degree** and a **doctorate**

▲ Studying science could take you to one of the most prestigious colleges or universities on the planet, such as the Massachusetts Institute of Technology (MIT) in Boston.

**STEM STANDS FOR SCIENCE, TECHNOLOGY, ENGINEERING, AND MATH. AS SCIENCE, TECHNOLOGY, AND ENGINEERING INDUSTRIES GROW, THERE IS INCREASING DEMAND FOR PEOPLE WITH STEM SKILLS.**

# PLANET HUNTER

**ARE YOU FASCINATED BY THE IDEA OF ALIEN LIFE? IF YOU ARE, THIS IS THE PERFECT JOB FOR YOU!**

An **exoplanet** is a planet orbiting a star other than our Sun. As an exoplanet hunter, you would search for these distant worlds, work out how large they are, and how they move around their stars. This tells us about how other solar systems in the universe work. Studying these other worlds also tells us whether there are other solar systems similar to our own, or whether ours is out of the ordinary in some way. More importantly, hunting for exoplanets will tell us how common Earth-like planets are, and what the chances are of alien life existing.

BY MAY 2016, SCIENTISTS HAD IDENTIFIED NEARLY 5,000 POTENTIAL EXOPLANETS. NEARLY HALF OF THESE HAD BEEN DISCOVERED USING THE KEPLER SPACE OBSERVATORY.

## WHAT YOU DO

As an exoplanet hunter, you would analyze data collected by some of the world's most powerful and sensitive telescopes. These telescopes, which are either in space, such as the Kepler Space Observatory (see right), or on Earth's surface, are pointed at thousands of stars in our galaxy. They detect the tiny changes in brightness as the planets pass in front of their stars, or if the star wobbles as the planet orbits it.

ASTROBIOLOGISTS STUDY EXOPLANETS TO SEE IF LIFE COULD SURVIVE ON THEM. AN ASTROBIOLOGIST IS AN EXPERT ON HOW LIFE CHANGES THE APPEARANCE OF A PLANET AND THE CHEMICALS IN ITS ATMOSPHERE.

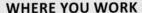

## WHERE YOU WORK

You would be working with a team of other scientists. This could be at a large **space agency**, such as NASA (National Aeronautics and Space Administration) or the ESA (European Space Agency), or in the astronomy department of a university. You would normally be in an office, but there would be opportunities to visit giant telescopes, which are often sited on remote mountaintops or in deserts.

**NASA**

**POST-SECONDARY:** Astrophysics, followed by research into stars and planets

▼ Launched in March 2009, the Kepler Space Observatory watches nearly 150,000 stars to see if they have exoplanets orbiting them.

**SECONDARY SCHOOL:** Physics and math, and possibly astronomy

▲ Exoplanets can be small, rocky worlds or huge gas giants, much bigger than Jupiter, the largest planet in our solar system.

# THE ROUTE TO PLANET HUNTING

YOU MAY NEED TO STUDY:

# CRIME FIGHTER

## THIS JOB USES CUTTING-EDGE SCIENCE TO SOLVE CRIMES AND CATCH THE BAD GUYS!

As a forensic scientist, you are trying to link criminal suspects to a crime. Forensic scientists help the police build a case to bring the suspects to court and have them **prosecuted**. No two cases are the same, so this job is always varied and interesting. Often, criminals accidentally leave evidence of their visit at the scene of a crime, or unwittingly take evidence from the scene with them. It's your job to search for this evidence at the scene and on suspects. Then you have to analyze the evidence and try to find matches between the suspect and the crime scene.

**FORENSIC** ANTHROPOLOGY **IS A SPECIAL BRANCH OF FORENSICS. FORENSIC ANTHROPOLOGISTS USE THEIR KNOWLEDGE OF ANATOMY TO BUILD A 3-D IMAGE OF WHAT A DEAD PERSON PROBABLY LOOKED LIKE, USING THEIR SKULL AS A STARTING POINT.**

▶ Forensic scientists catalogue and collect all sorts of evidence, such as footprints, fibers from clothing, and traces of saliva.

# WHAT YOU DO

What you do each day depends on the stage of a crime case, and your particular role in an investigation. At the start of a case, you might visit the scene of the crime to search for and collect evidence. This has to be carefully packaged and labeled. Most of the time, you would be based in a forensic laboratory, using test equipment to analyze samples. This could involve looking at fibers under a microscope, analyzing the different chemicals in a speck of paint, or sending a sample of blood to a laboratory for its DNA to be analyzed. At the end of a case, you might be called to a court of law to act as an **expert witness**, telling the court about the evidence that you've found. So you need to be sure of your facts!

▼ Many police forces have special labs set up for their forensic teams.

## WHERE YOU WORK

As a forensic scientist, you would work for the police service in your country, in the forensic science department, or for a company that does forensic work for the police. Forensic scientists also work for fire services, helping to find out what caused a fire, or the armed forces to investigate crimes involving military personnel.

YOU MAY NEED TO STUDY:

# THE ROUTE

**SECONDARY SCHOOL:**
Physics and chemistry

# TO FORENSIC

**POST-SECONDARY:**
Chemistry, biology, or medical science

# SCIENCE

**AFTER POST-SECONDARY:**
Specialized training in forensics

# FEEDING THE WORLD

## THIS JOB MAKES SURE THAT THE FOOD YOU EAT IS SAFE, NUTRITIONAL, AND TASTY.

You only have to look at the ingredients and the information on food packaging to see that a great deal of science is involved in preparing your food. Food scientists use their knowledge of chemistry to develop tasty new things to eat and drink, and improve the quality and taste of other food and drink products. Food scientists also find out how to make food and drinks more quickly and cheaply, and how to make them last longer on supermarket shelves.

## WHAT YOU DO

▼ Testing food to make sure it is safe and free from germs is a key part of a food scientist's job.

As a food scientist, you would work in a laboratory most of the time, trying different combinations of ingredients to create new foods. You might also organize tasting sessions to see how customers like the flavors of new products. If you are working in food production, you would spend time in a factory, carrying out quality and safety tests on finished products.

## THE ROUTE TO FOOD SCIENCE

YOU MAY NEED TO STUDY:

▲ Governments have their own food testing labs, such as this one in Australia.

## WHERE YOU WORK

There are plenty of opportunities for food scientists, as there are thousands of companies producing food and drinks in most countries. These can range from small bakeries and chocolatiers to huge companies producing millions of ready meals for supermarkets. Some food scientists also work for local authorities as hygiene inspectors, taking samples of food from stores and restaurants to make sure they are safe to eat.

▲ Food scientists also calculate the **nutritional information** that goes on food packaging, so that shoppers can make an informed decision about their diet.

**POST-SECONDARY:**
A degree in food science

**SECONDARY SCHOOL:**
Science, especially chemistry

 A FOOD FLAVORIST USES CHEMISTRY TO CREATE DELICIOUS TASTES BY COMBINING DIFFERENT INGREDIENTS AND CHEMICALS. FLAVORISTS WORK FOR COMPANIES CALLED FLAVOR HOUSES.

# WORKING IN SPACE

## GET READY TO BLAST OFF WITH A JOB THAT IS TRULY OUT OF THIS WORLD.

As well as the thrill of living in space, and having an incredible view of Earth, astronauts push the boundaries of science and technology. A mission specialist is an astronaut who carries out a particular scientific or technical job in space. Each mission specialist has a list of jobs to do. These jobs include conducting a range of science experiments, such as testing how plants grow, or how crystals form in the low gravity of Earth's orbit. Other jobs include helping to maintain and repair the International Space Station (ISS).

▲ An astronaut admires the view from the International Space Station.

## WHAT YOU DO

As an astronaut, you will spend most of your time on Earth, training for your time in space. Once in space, you will sleep, eat, and work on a strict timetable. An important part of your day will be exercising on special machines to prevent your muscles from becoming weak in orbit.

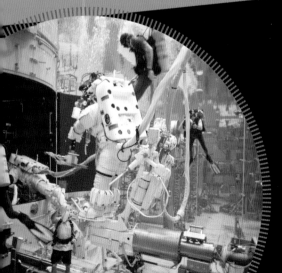

◄ Training for a spacewalk involves many practice sessions underwater in a large pool back on Earth.

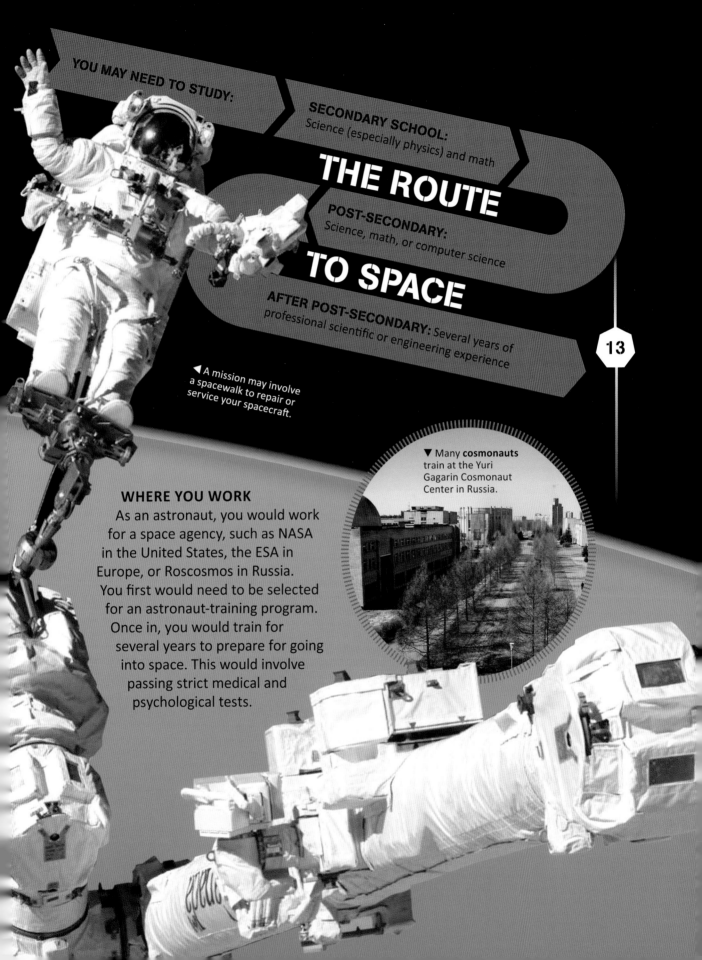

**SECONDARY SCHOOL:**
Science (especially physics) and math

# THE ROUTE

**POST-SECONDARY:**
Science, math, or computer science

# TO SPACE

**AFTER POST-SECONDARY:** Several years of
professional scientific or engineering experience

◀ A mission may involve
a spacewalk to repair or
service your spacecraft.

13

▼ Many **cosmonauts**
train at the Yuri
Gagarin Cosmonaut
Center in Russia.

## WHERE YOU WORK

As an astronaut, you would work
for a space agency, such as NASA
in the United States, the ESA in
Europe, or Roscosmos in Russia.
You first would need to be selected
for an astronaut-training program.
Once in, you would train for
several years to prepare for going
into space. This would involve
passing strict medical and
psychological tests.

# FIXING THE BRAIN

14

▶ A team of surgeons operate on a patient's brain.

## THIS JOB LETS YOU DELVE INTO THE MOST COMPLICATED MACHINE IN THE UNIVERSE—THE HUMAN BRAIN.

Being a **neurosurgeon** is one of the most challenging jobs in medicine. It requires amazing skills, takes extensive training, and is very challenging. But it offers a huge amount of satisfaction in helping patients and saving lives. Neurosurgeons treat patients who have problems with their **nervous systems**. They analyze what problems a patient has, decide whether they can fix them with an operation, and perform surgery if needed.

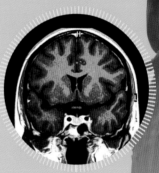

▲ Surgeons can study the inside of the brain using special scanners.

## THE ROUTE TO NEUROSURGERY

YOU MAY NEED TO STUDY:

SECONDARY SCHO
Biology and chemistry

**CARDIOTHORACIC SURGERY INVOLVES THE HEART, LUNGS, AND CHEST, INCLUDING CORRECTING HEART DEFECTS SUCH AS DAMAGED VALVES, AND HEART AND LUNG TRANSPLANTS.**

YOUR BRAIN MAKES UP ABOUT 2 PERCENT OF YOUR WEIGHT, BUT USES 20 PERCENT OF YOUR BODY'S ENERGY.

# WHAT YOU DO

As a neurosurgeon, you might have consultations with new patients to discuss their problems, organize tests for them (such as blood tests and scans), decide treatment plans, and explain the plans to the patients. You would also do ward rounds, checking up on patients who are already undergoing treatment. You might also consult with a team to decide whether a particular patient needs surgery, and supervise more junior doctors. You would work in the operating room several hours a week, performing delicate surgeries.

**POST-SECONDARY:**
Medical science

**AFTER POST-SECONDARY:** Five years general medical training, followed by up to ten years of specialized training while working as a doctor

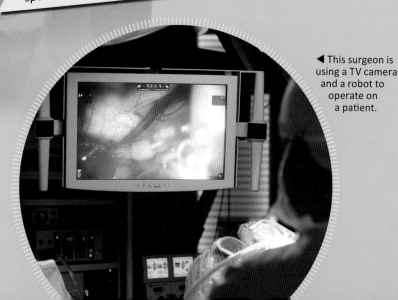

◄ This surgeon is using a TV camera and a robot to operate on a patient.

## WHERE YOU WORK
You would normally work in a large hospital, possibly one that specializes in neurosurgery. Alternatively, you could work for a private health company.

# PENGUIN COUNTER

THE LARGEST PENGUIN COLONY CONTAINS ABOUT TWO MILLION CHINSTRAP PENGUINS. IT IS FOUND IN THE SOUTH SANDWICH ISLANDS.

**THIS SCIENCE JOB WILL TAKE YOU TO THE ENDS OF THE EARTH WHERE YOU CAN STUDY THE HEALTH OF OUR PLANET.**

16

A few scientists are lucky enough to work in some of the world's most beautiful places, including the polar regions. As a polar scientist, you might study the climate, rocks, glaciers, or the local wildlife. This work is important, as the changing numbers of penguins and other animals that live near the poles may be linked to human activities, and specifically to global warming. Penguin researchers collect data, including how many birds live in each colony and how the numbers change over time. They attach small digital cameras and micro **GPS** trackers to some penguins to monitor their movements.

## WHAT YOU DO

Counting penguins normally means leaving the cozy warmth of a polar base and living in a tent for weeks or even months, counting birds each day. The cold and wind, even in the Antarctic summer, make for difficult working and living conditions. But being in one of the world's most beautiful places would offset these hardships. You will also spend time back at the base analyzing data.

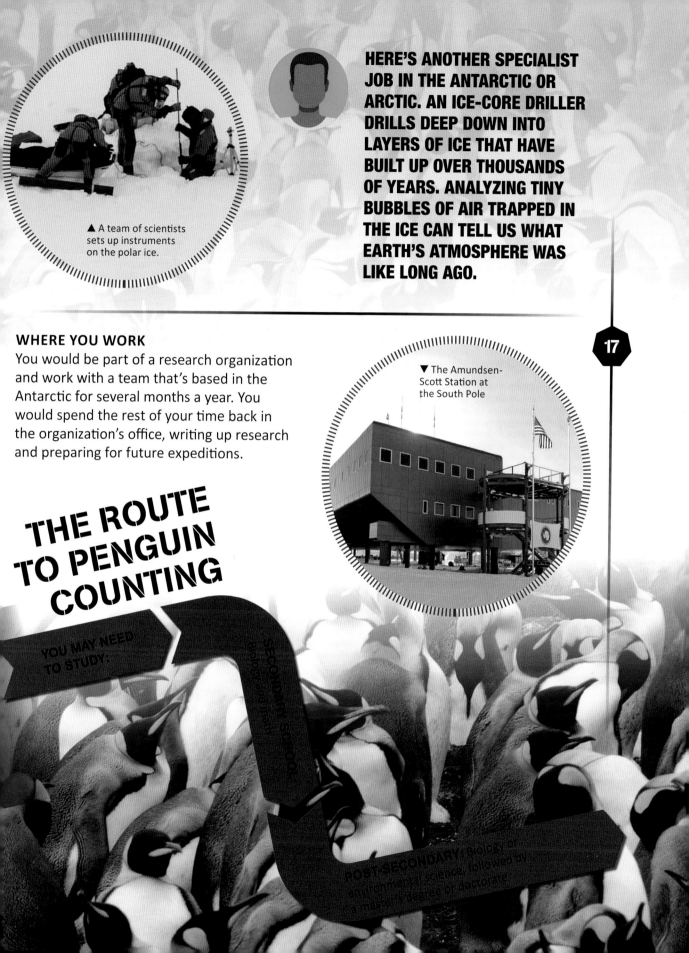

HERE'S ANOTHER SPECIALIST JOB IN THE ANTARCTIC OR ARCTIC. AN ICE-CORE DRILLER DRILLS DEEP DOWN INTO LAYERS OF ICE THAT HAVE BUILT UP OVER THOUSANDS OF YEARS. ANALYZING TINY BUBBLES OF AIR TRAPPED IN THE ICE CAN TELL US WHAT EARTH'S ATMOSPHERE WAS LIKE LONG AGO.

▲ A team of scientists sets up instruments on the polar ice.

## WHERE YOU WORK

You would be part of a research organization and work with a team that's based in the Antarctic for several months a year. You would spend the rest of your time back in the organization's office, writing up research and preparing for future expeditions.

▼ The Amundsen-Scott Station at the South Pole

# THE ROUTE TO PENGUIN COUNTING

YOU MAY NEED TO STUDY:

SECONDARY SCHOOL: Biology and math

POST-SECONDARY: Biology or environmental science, followed by a master's degree or doctorate

# STORM TRACKER

## THIS JOB LETS YOU GET CLOSE TO SOME OF THE MOST VIOLENT EVENTS ON THE PLANET.

Storm trackers are **meteorologists** who follow the progress of powerful storms, including **hurricanes**, **tornadoes**, and huge thunderstorms. They help us to predict dangerous storms and save lives by warning people to get out of the way. Storm trackers monitor data from weather stations, images from satellites, and forecasts calculated by computers. This allows them to predict where storms may strike. Storm trackers occasionally study storms up close. They might put themselves in the path of a hurricane or tornado to measure wind speeds and take photos.

▲ The winds in a tornado can reach speeds of more than 280 mph (450 kph).

THERE ARE ABOUT 1,000 TORNADOES EVERY YEAR ON AVERAGE IN THE UNITED STATES ALONE, AND ABOUT 100 IN CANADA.

## WHAT YOU DO

As a storm tracker, you spend most of your time in an office, tracking hurricanes on a computer or watching the development of storms that create floods or tornadoes. You might have to contact the media with storm warnings. On some days, you might leave the office to collect data from the storm itself. In the case of a tornado, you'll be in a specially built truck equipped with **radar** wind-speed measuring equipment.

A FEW ORGANIZATIONS OPERATE HURRICANE-HUNTING AIRCRAFT, CREWED BY PILOTS AND METEOROLOGISTS. THESE FLY RIGHT INTO HURRICANES TO COLLECT DATA ON THEIR SIZE AND STRENGTH.

YOU MAY NEED TO STUDY:

# THE ROUTE TO

**POST-SECONDARY:**
Meteorology

**SECONDARY SCHOOL:**
Science and math

# STORM TRACKING

**AFTER POST-SECONDARY:**
Gain experience in general meteorology before specializing in storm tracking

▲ This photo was taken from a plane flying inside the eye of a hurricane.

▼ A team of tornado trackers monitors a nearby storm.

## WHERE YOU WORK

You would normally be working for a country's official meteorological organization, such as the NOAA (National Oceanic and Atmospheric Administration) in the United States or the CMOS (Canadian Meteorological and Oceanographic Society) in Canada. There are also some private weather-watching companies you could work for. A few people work for themselves as "storm chasers." They try to get as close as they can to hurricanes and tornadoes for the thrill of seeing these wild storms close up, and to make some money by selling videos and photographs. This can be very dangerous!

# PREDICTING ERUPTIONS

## THIS JOB MAY HAVE YOU PLAYING WITH FIRE, BUT IT'S VITAL TO PREDICTING ERUPTIONS AND SAVING LIVES!

**Volcanologists** observe volcanoes that are erupting, and monitor volcanoes that are **dormant**. They collect samples of ash and lava and record volcanic activity from hour to hour. They look for signs that dormant volcanoes are about to erupt again. These include the ground bulging, gases spewing from the volcano's vent, and small earthquakes that show that **magma** is moving deep underground. Volcanologists also look at the old lava flows and deposits of ash, which show them how volcanoes erupted in the past.

## WHAT YOU DO

You will spend some time each day collecting data from instruments that you have set up on a volcano, such as **seismometers** and GPS sensors, then analyzing the results. You will need to wear protection against the heat for collecting lava samples.

◀ As a volcanologist, you might have to get very close to the action to collect samples!

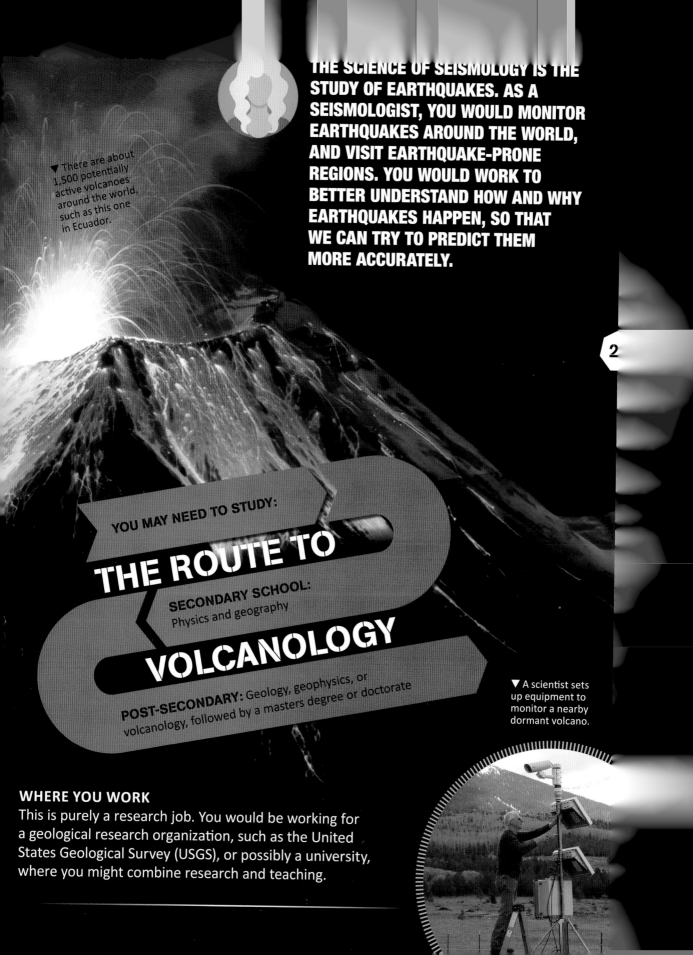

▼ There are about 1,500 potentially active volcanoes around the world, such as this one in Ecuador.

THE SCIENCE OF SEISMOLOGY IS THE STUDY OF EARTHQUAKES. AS A SEISMOLOGIST, YOU WOULD MONITOR EARTHQUAKES AROUND THE WORLD, AND VISIT EARTHQUAKE-PRONE REGIONS. YOU WOULD WORK TO BETTER UNDERSTAND HOW AND WHY EARTHQUAKES HAPPEN, SO THAT WE CAN TRY TO PREDICT THEM MORE ACCURATELY.

YOU MAY NEED TO STUDY:

# THE ROUTE TO

**SECONDARY SCHOOL:** Physics and geography

# VOLCANOLOGY

**POST-SECONDARY:** Geology, geophysics, or volcanology, followed by a masters degree or doctorate

▼ A scientist sets up equipment to monitor a nearby dormant volcano.

## WHERE YOU WORK

This is purely a research job. You would be working for a geological research organization, such as the United States Geological Survey (USGS), or possibly a university, where you might combine research and teaching.

# GENETIC ENGINEER

## SOME SCIENTISTS WORK WITH THE TINY BUILDING BLOCKS OF LIFE, CALLED GENES, TO CHANGE PLANT AND ANIMAL SPECIES.

**DNA**, or deoxyribonucleic acid, is a substance that's found in almost every cell in animals and plants. A gene is a chunk of DNA that controls how a particular cell grows and what it does. Genetic engineers work with DNA to alter the characteristics of plants and animals. For example, they might replace a gene in one species of plant with a gene from another species to make the first plant grow faster or become more resistant to disease. Any new species made like this is known as **genetically modified** (GM).

◄ The plant below has been altered to make it resistant to the disease that has damaged the plant above.

▲ These pet fish have been genetically altered to make them glow.

## WHAT YOU DO

As a genetic engineer, you would spend most of your time in a **biotechnology** laboratory. You would use very specialized equipment and chemicals to analyze samples of DNA, to copy pieces of DNA, to chop up DNA, and to replace genes in cells with genes from other cells. You would also be looking after plants and animals in the lab. Outside the lab, you would keep up to date with the latest developments in genetic engineering techniques, and even publish you own scientific papers.

# THE ROUTE

YOU MAY NEED TO STUDY:

## TO GENETIC

**SECONDARY SCHOOL:**
Biology, chemistry, and math

## ENGINEERING

**POST-SECONDARY:** Biotechnology, biochemistry, or genetics

## WHERE YOU WORK

You have a choice of working for research organizations, universities, or biotechnology companies. There are an increasing number of opportunities as the science of genetic engineering becomes more widely used.

▶ This scientist is checking how well a crop of genetically modified corn is growing at a research station.

# BRINGING THE PAST TO LIFE

## THE STUDY OF EXTINCT SPECIES CAN REVEAL WHAT LIFE WAS LIKE MILLIONS OF YEARS AGO.

Dinosaurology is the study of dinosaurs. It involves unearthing fossil remains and studying them in close detail. It is an exciting job, but don't get it confused with being a fossil hunter. You might have seen fossil hunters unearthing dinosaur bones from the desert in TV documentaries, and even in the movies, but dinosaurologists do much more! Dinosaurologists and **paleontologists** are experts in the anatomy of plants and animals, and also geology.

A NEW SPECIES OF DINOSAUR IS REVEALED APPROXIMATELY EVERY TWO WEEKS, EITHER STRAIGHT OUT OF THE GROUND, OR HIDDEN IN AN OLD COLLECTION.

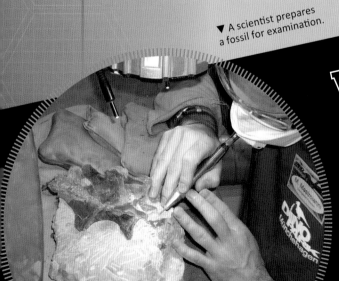

▼ A scientist prepares a fossil for examination.

## WHAT YOU DO

As a dinosaurologist, you would spend most of your time in a laboratory or office analyzing fossils, writing descriptions of them, trying to identify them, and working out what species of dinosaur (or other animal) they belong to. You might also teach students about paleontology. You could do **fieldwork** for a few weeks each year, carefully digging dinosaur fossils from the ground.

## YOU MAY NEED TO STUDY:

## THE ROUTE TO

**SECONDARY SCHOOL:** Science (especially biology) and geography

## DINOSAUROLOGY

**POST-SECONDARY:** Geology, anatomy or earth sciences, along with experience of fieldwork, followed by a doctorate

## WHERE YOU WORK

There are no commercial organizations that employ dinosaurologists, so you would be working for research organizations or universities researching newly discovered species of dinosaurs.

25

▲ By studying fossils, scientists can piece together entire skeletons and work out how dinosaurs lived.

PALEOBOTANISTS STUDY THE FOSSILS OF ANCIENT PLANTS. THESE REMAINS TELL US WHAT PLANTS LIVED ON EARTH IN THE PAST, AND GIVE US AN IDEA OF HOW EARTH MIGHT HAVE LOOKED.

# RUN FASTER!

**THIS JOB HELPS ATHLETES TO RUN FASTER, JUMP HIGHER, AND PERFORM AT THEIR VERY BEST.**

A biomechanist can make a difference in the performance of athletes. Even small changes in technique can be the difference between winning and losing. **Biomechanics** is the study of motion and the forces producing motion. Biomechanists also learn about bones, joints, and muscles, and how they work together. They apply this specialized knowledge to help athletes move more efficiently, so they can run and swim faster, throw farther, and jump higher. They also help athletes to avoid getting injured.

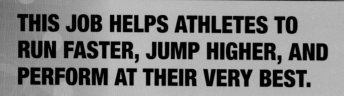

▲ Improving her technique means that this athlete can jump even farther.

▲ Analyzing an athlete's **gait**, or stride, can improve a runner's speed and efficiency.

## WHAT YOU DO

As a biomechanist, you would spend some of your day in a lab using special equipment to study athletes. High-speed cameras help study how a person moves. Measuring tools help gauge the strength and performance of different muscles. You would analyze results and advise athletes on how to improve their techniques.

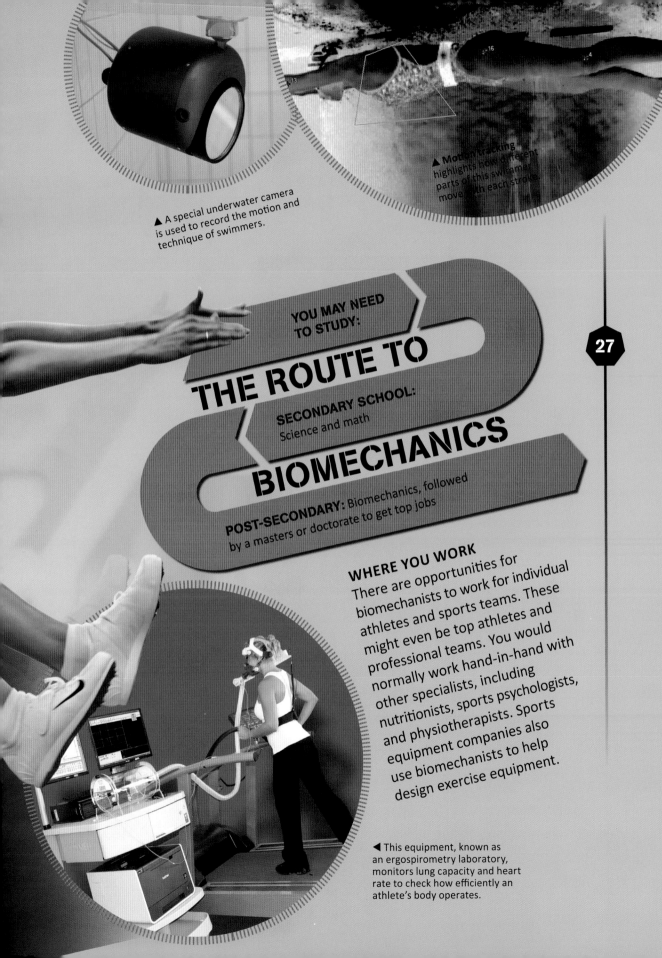

▲ A special underwater camera is used to record the motion and technique of swimmers.

▲ Motion tracking highlights how different parts of this swimmer move with each stroke.

**YOU MAY NEED TO STUDY:**

# THE ROUTE TO

**SECONDARY SCHOOL:** Science and math

# BIOMECHANICS

**POST-SECONDARY:** Biomechanics, followed by a masters or doctorate to get top jobs

## WHERE YOU WORK

There are opportunities for biomechanists to work for individual athletes and sports teams. These might even be top athletes and professional teams. You would normally work hand-in-hand with other specialists, including nutritionists, sports psychologists, and physiotherapists. Sports equipment companies also use biomechanists to help design exercise equipment.

◄ This equipment, known as an ergospirometry laboratory, monitors lung capacity and heart rate to check how efficiently an athlete's body operates.

# ATOM SMASHER

▼ When particles smash into each other, they break up into tiny particles that can be detected by sensors.

## BY SMASHING THINGS APART, THIS JOB COULD HELP YOU UNCOVER THE SECRETS OF THE UNIVERSE.

Particle physicists smash **atoms** apart in an attempt to discover what stuff is exactly made from. There are two types of particle physicist. Theoretical particle physicists come up with theories about what particles they think exist. Experimental particle physicists develop experiments to test those theories!

▼ Physicists at the Large Hadron Collider study data after a collision.

## WHAT YOU DO

As a theoretical particle physicist, you would spend your time in an office at a university working on theories using computer models and a pen and paper. You might also pass on your expertise by lecturing students. As an experimental particle physicist, you would spend some days performing experiments. Other days will be spent analyzing results and writing reports, or developing and building new experimental machines.

## WHERE YOU WORK

All particle physicists work for universities or research organizations. You might work for many years as part of a team researching a particular problem. As an experimental physicist, you would work at an experimental facility, such as the Large Hadron Collider (LHC) in Switzerland and France.

**POST-SECONDARY:** Physics or astrophysics, followed by research and a master's degree or doctorate in particle physics

THE CIRCULAR TUNNEL AT THE LARGE HADRON COLLIDER HAS A CIRCUMFERENCE OF 17 MILES (27 KM).

**SECONDARY SCHOOL:** Science (especially physics and chemistry) and math

# THE ROUTE TO PARTICLE PHYSICS

YOU MAY NEED TO STUDY:

◄ Tiny atoms are sent along the tunnels at close to the speed of light.

◄ The large tunnel of the LHC runs underground on the border between France and Switzerland.

# GLOSSARY

**ANTHROPOLOGY**
The study of human culture, including our origins, religious beliefs, and how we relate socially with each other

**ATOM**
A tiny particle that is usually made up of a nucleus containing protons and neutrons, with one or more electrons whizzing around them

**BIOMECHANICS**
The study of how living things move about, including how people walk, run, and jump

**BIOTECHNOLOGY**
Using tiny organisms, such as bacteria, to carry out chemical changes, such as producing medicines or food

**COSMONAUT**
The Russian name given to a person who travels into space

**DNA**
Short for deoxyribonucleic acid; This strand-like chemical is found inside cells and contains the code which tells the cell how to grow and behave.

**DOCTORATE**
One of the highest education qualifications students can receive

**DORMANT**
A volcano that hasn't erupted for a period of time, but that might erupt at some point in the future

**EXOPLANET**
A planet that orbits a star other than our Sun

**EXPERT WITNESS**
A person who is specialized in a particular subject and gives his or her expert opinion in court

**FIELDWORK**
The collection of data outside of a classroom, laboratory, or office

**GAIT**
How a person walks or runs

**GENES**
Parts of the DNA that are passed from parents to their offspring, and give a specific characteristic, such as how a living thing behaves or looks

**GENETICALLY MODIFIED**
When the genes of an organism have been altered to change one of its characteristics

**GPS**
Short for Global Positioning System; This is a network of satellites in orbit around Earth, which a person can use to locate their position with a receiver.

**HURRICANES**
Huge tropical storms that form over oceans

**MAGMA**
Liquid rock that swirls beneath Earth's surface in a layer called the mantle

## MASTER'S DEGREE
A university degree that is a higher level than a bachelor's degree

## METEOROLOGIST
A person who studies the weather and how it is created by events in Earth's atmosphere

## MOTION TRACKING
Following and recording the movement of an object or parts of a person's body to see how they behave

## NERVOUS SYSTEM
The system of nerve cells that carry small electrical signals around an organism; It also includes the spinal cord and brain.

## NEUROSURGEON
A person who performs surgery on a patient's nervous system

## NUTRITIONAL INFORMATION
The data, usually found on packaging, which tells you what nutrients are inside food

## PALEONTOLOGIST
A scientist who studies the fossil remains of long-dead plants and animals to find out how they lived and what conditions were like when they were alive

## PROSECUTED
When someone has been charged with a criminal act and taken to court

## RADAR
A system to locate objects, such as planes and boats, which uses a beam of radio signals and detects the echoes of this beam to calculate the location

## SEISMOMETER
Also called a seismograph; This is a device which records earthquakes, measuring their magnitude.

## SPACE AGENCY
An organization that sends robot or crewed missions into space

## TORNADOES
Powerful storms that form funnel-shaped clouds as they spin around violently

## TRANSPLANT
In surgery, this is the removal of one body part that is sick or has stopped working, and replacing it with a new part that has usually been taken from a live donor or a person who recently died.

## UNDERGRADUATE
A person who is studying at a university for their first degree

## VOLCANOLOGIST
A scientist who studies volcanoes and their eruptions

# INDEX